MULTI-CAREERING

FRAMES
BARNA GROUP

MULTI-CAREERING

Do Work That Matters at Every Stage of Your Journey

BOB GOFF
RE/FRAMES BY SCOTT HARRISON
AND KEATON RANNOW

ZONDERVAN

Multi-Careering
Copyright © 2013 by Barna Group

This title is also available as a Zondervan ebook.
Visit www.zondervan.com/ebooks.

This title is also available in a Zondervan audio edition.
Visit www.zondervan.fm.

Requests for information should be addressed to:

Zondervan, *Grand Rapids, Michigan 49530*

ISBN 978-0-310-43334-7 (softcover)

Published in association with the literary agency of The Fedd Agency, Inc,
401 Ranch Road 620 South, Suite 350c, Austin, TX 78734.

Cover design and interior graphics: Amy Duty
Interior design: Kate Mulvaney

Printed in the United States of America

13 14 15 16 17 18 /DCI/ 18 17 16 15 14 13 12 11 10 9 8 7 6 5 4 3 2

CONTENTS

WHY YOU NEED FRAMES

These days, you probably find yourself with less time than ever.

Everything seems like it's moving at a faster pace—except your ability to keep up.

Somehow, you are weighed down with more obligations than you have ever had before.

Life feels more complicated. More complex.

If you're like most people, you probably have lots of questions about how to live a life that matters. You feel as though you have more to learn than can possibly be learned. But with smaller chunks of time and more sources of information than ever before, where can you turn for real insight and livable wisdom?

Barna Group has produced this series to examine the complicated issues of life and to help you live more meaningfully. We call it FRAMES—like a good set of eyeglasses that help you see the world more clearly ... or a work of art perfectly hung that invites you to look more closely ... or a building's skeleton, the part that is most essential to its structure.

The FRAMES Season 1 collection provides thoughtful and concise, data-driven and visually appealing insights for anyone who wants a more faith-driven and fulfilling life. In each FRAME we couple new cultural analysis from our team at Barna with an essay from leading voices in the field, providing information and ideas for you to digest in a more easily consumed number of words.

After all, it's a fast-paced world, full of words and images vying for your attention. Most of us have a number of half-read or "read someday" books on our shelves. But each FRAME aims to give you the essential information and real-life application behind one of today's most crucial trends in less than one-quarter the length of most books. These are big ideas in small books— designed so you truly can read less but know more. And the infographics and ideas in this FRAME are intended for share-ability. So read it, then find someone to "frame" with these ideas, and keep the conversation going (see "Share This Frame" on page 86).

Furthermore, each FRAME brings a distinctly Christian point of view to today's trends. In times of uncertainty, people look for guides. And we believe the Christian community is trying to make sense of the dramatic social changes happening around us.

Over the past thirty years, Barna Group has built a reputation as a trusted analyst of religion and culture. We offer cultural discernment for the Christian community by thoughtful analysts who care enough to tell the truth about what's really happening in today's society.

So sit back, but not for long. With FRAMES we invite you to read less and know more.

DAVID KINNAMAN
FRAMES, executive producer
president / Barna Group

ROXANNE STONE
FRAMES, general editor
vice president / Barna Group

Learn more at www.barnaframes.com.

F R A M E S

TITLE	20 and Something	Becoming Home	Fighting for Peace	Greater Expectations
PURPOSE	Have the Time of Your Life (And Figure It All Out Too)	Adoption, Foster Care, and Mentoring – Living Out God's Heart for Orphans	Your Role in a Culture Too Comfortable with Violence	Succeed (and Stay Sane) in an On-Demand, All-Access, Always-On Age
AUTHOR	David H. Kim	Jedd Medefind	Carol Howard Merritt & Tyler Wigg-Stevenson	Claire Diaz-Ortiz
KEY TREND	27% of young adults have clear goals for the next 5 years	62% of Americans believe Christians have a responsibility to adopt	47% of adults say they're less comfortable with violence than 10 years ago	42% of people are unhappy with their work/ life balance

PERFECT FOR SMALL GROUP DISCUSSION

FRAMES Season 1: DVD
FRAMES Season 1: The Complete Collection

READ LESS.
KNOW MORE.

The Hyperlinked Life	Multi-Careering	Sacred Roots	Schools in Crisis	Wonder Women
Live with Wisdom in an Age of Information Overload	Do Work That Matters at Every Stage of Your Journey	Why the Church Still Matters	They Need Your Help (Whether You Have Kids or Not)	Navigating the Challenges of Motherhood, Career, and Identity
Jun Young & David Kinnaman	Bob Goff	Jon Tyson	Nicole Baker Fulgham	Kate Harris
71% of adults admit they're overwhelmed by information	75% of adults are looking for ways to live a more meaningful life	51% of people don't think it's important to attend church	46% of Americans say public schools are worse than 5 years ago	72% of women say they're stressed

#BarnaFrames

www.barnaframes.com

BEFORE YOU READ

....

- What would you say is the difference between a job and a career?

- Do you think it's better to have one career or multiple careers? Why?

- Would you say your work-life balance is good? What would you change?

- What are your priorities for your career? What are the top three things you want out of a job?

- Is your job meaningful? Do you feel like you're doing good in the world as you work? If not, would you say it's because of the work you do or the way you approach that work?

- Do you think you will be able to retire someday? Do you want to? What will you do if you no longer have to earn an income?

- If you could do anything for a career, what would it be? What is the first step toward that goal?

MULTI-CAREERING

Do Work That Matters at Every Stage of Your Journey

INFOGRAPHICS

The game of

L I F E

YOUNG ADULT

CAREER

FAMILY

"My work is creating a better world": 1/4 of Christian Millennials

Financial Independence: 59% rank this as the top goal of 20s

Not Completing Education: top regret from 20s

1 in 3 Christians: feel called to their current work

77% of adults: desire a clear purpose for living

"I feel overcommitted at work": 30% of adults

3/5 adults: "Family is my top priority"

"My marriage makes me very happy": 54% of adults

Family: the #1 area of satisfaction for most people

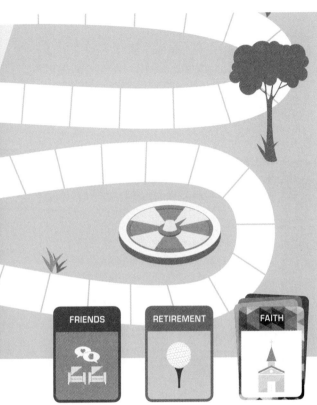

Friends Forever:
49% have a friend they can talk to about anything

1 in 3 adults:
often feel lonely

Networked:
36% have a strong support network of friends and family

62% of adults:
expect to work after retirement

Retirement = more time with family:
3/4 of adults

22% of Boomers:
plan to volunteer after they retire

Self-Help: Church is #1 area people want to improve

Priorities: Elders are most likely to rank church as their top priority

"Church offers me emotional support":
37% of all adults

The search for

MEANING

What is the point of life? As you might expect,
it's a question most people are asking. Whether or not
they're finding answers is a little less certain.

1/2 *of adults are searching for
meaning and purpose in life*

1/8 *say they are unclear about
that meaning and purpose*

*75% are looking for ways
to live a more meaningful life*

56%	46%	25%	20%
want to make a difference in the world	are afraid of making the wrong career choice	have clear goals for where they want to be in 5 years	have a sense of what God wants them to do with their life

Among all adults

WHAT YOU DO

$$\neq$$

who you are

"What do you do?" It's often the first question we ask one another. So does our meaning come from our jobs? Most adults would say "no" … in fact, when asked what's central to their identity, adults rank career last.

63%
FAMILY

46%
PERSONAL INTERESTS

39%
FAITH

34%
FRIENDS

32%
CAREER

Even so, adults spend the most amount of time at work …

- Church: **6%**
- Friends: **7%**
- Personal time: **16%**
- Career: **36%**
- Family: **35%**

And desire a job they're passionate about …

- Passion: **39%**
- Financial security: **33%**
- Funds personal life: **28%**

MULTI-CAREERING

Do Work That Matters at Every Stage of Your Journey

FRAMEWORK

BY BARNA GROUP

Richard "Dick" Kyker went to work as a sheriff's deputy in Kern County, California, in 1963. He had gone to Korea with the Marines, then worked in an oil refinery for a few years, but now Dick was married with two school-age daughters and an infant son; it was time to settle down and raise the kids.

Dick worked minimum security at Lerdo Detention Facility, running the shop where inmates fixed the trucks, cars, and vans in the Sheriff's Department fleet. While Dick may have been an officer of the law, at heart he was a mechanic. He loved anything with four wheels and four or more cylinders. (He had, in fact, raced stock cars as a younger man until his wife, whom everybody called Boots, put her foot down.)

Dick retired in his early sixties, having worked for the department for over thirty years. He had a full pension from the county and had been a scrupulous manager of his family's finances through the years, saving and investing so there would be plenty to live on over and above Social Security. He and Boots took Alaskan and Caribbean cruises, vacationed in Hawaii, explored Irish castles and the Australian outback, and went on safari in East Africa. He took up golf and bought himself a '32 Ford Roadster to tinker with in the garage. Dick and Boots also had a hand in raising their grandchildren.

Dick's is certainly not an uncommon story — especially among Americans of his generation. A decent paying job in the public or private sector, good benefits, and a nice retirement after thirty or forty years at the company, with plenty of time to enjoy grandchildren, adventure, and personal hobbies.

It *wasn't* an uncommon story. But in the coming years —and for the coming generations—it's a story that seems increasingly unlikely. And, for many, increasingly undesirable.

A Changed Landscape

Nearly half of today's working adults over the age of 50 (46%) believe they will not be able to retire as early as their parents, and nearly two-thirds (62%) assume they will work even after they retire from their current career. Of those who expect to do at least some work after they retire, nearly three-quarters (73%) say they'll work because they *want* to. And many imagine doing a new type of work—nearly three in ten (29%) expect to venture outside their industry after retirement.

But long before they contemplate retirement in their sixties or seventies (or eighties), American workers in younger generations face a vastly different employment landscape than when Dick Kyker went to work in 1963. For a variety of reasons—including the loss of manufacturing jobs to overseas workers, the decline of workers' unions, and the rise of the freelancer—it is no longer common to work throughout your career for the same employer. While there are still public-sector jobs, such as sheriff's deputy, that offer workers long-term security (albeit without the pension), today's average job tenure is just four and half years. That's about one-eighth of Dick's tenure with the Sheriff's Department.

And for younger generations, the time drops even more. According to a Future Workplace survey more than

WHEN I RETIRE I WANT TO ...

Spend time with family

76%

Pursue personal hobbies

57%

Adventure

42%

Volunteer

23%

Use my skills in a new line of work

19%

Own my own business

15%

A "RETIRED" APPROACH TO WORK
I EXPECT TO DO ...

- Little to no work after I retire: **38%**
- At least a little work in my current industry: **33%**
- At least a little work, but in a new industry: **29%**

 73% say they'll work because they want to

 27% say they'll work because they need to

46% of adults over 50 believe they'll retire later than their parents

Among unretired adults

90% of Millennials expect to stay at their current job less than three years.

Where once a twentysomething might easily have answered the question, "Where will you be in five years?" with a checklist of expectations — a higher position in my company, a house with a decent mortgage and a large yard, a spouse, kids — today's twentysomething isn't so sure. In fact, only about a quarter of Millennials (27%) have clear goals for where they want to be in five years or would even express confidence in their current life choices (26%). Less than one in five (19%) say they're extremely satisfied with their current work. (For more on how the Millennials are redefining what it means to be in your twenties, see the Barna FRAME *20 and Something* by David H. Kim.)

These trends don't apply only to Millennials. A similar number of all adults (25%) are unsure of where they'll be in five years. While about four in ten Elders (38%) express confidence in their current life choices, Gen Xers and Boomers aren't feeling much better than Millennials.

"I'm confident in my current life choices"

26%	Millennials
30%	Gen-Xers
30%	Boomers
38%	Elders

The young and the restless

Millennials are just starting to figure out what career looks like. And many of them still have a lot of questions.

27%

have clear
goals for where
they want to be
in 5 years

Average tenure
of American
employee per job*

4.4
years of service

26%

are very
confident in
their current
life choices

<3
years of service

How long **91%**
of Millennials
expect to stay
in a single job**

19%

are extremely
satisfied
with their work
or career

*Source: Bureau of Labor Statistics
**Source: Future Workplace, "Multiple Generations @ Work"

So, what does all this mean? For one thing, it means career fluidity. Among twentysomethings, Gen Xers, and even Boomers, multi-careering is the new normal.

The Multi in Multi-Careering

We made up the word *multi-careering*. We hope it will catch on because so far we haven't come across anything better that accurately describes this modern phenomenon. In previous decades, American workers perfected multitasking. Today's economy demands multi-careering. And while the circumstances that may have led some to pursue a second (or third or fourth) career are not always positive, there are plenty of opportunities to embrace in this new multi-careering landscape.

A great example of multi-careering is Katie Davis, founder of Amazima Ministries International and author of *Kisses from Katie*.

As an eighteen-year-old, Katie visited Uganda for the first time. Two years later she moved to Uganda and founded Amazima, which matches orphaned children with sponsors around the world to provide schooling, school supplies, three hot meals a day, minor medical care, and spiritual encouragement. She imports handmade jewelry to the United States, helping Ugandan mothers provide for their families. She has adopted thirteen orphaned girls. She wrote a book to tell her story and raise support for her work. Katie is twenty-six years old — a mother thirteen times over, a best-selling author, an import entrepreneur, and the founder of an international ministry.

Another example is Chuck, a father of four in his early forties who has done everything from selling vacuums and burial plots to shooting and editing commercials. His day job is graphic design for a large marketing firm, but Chuck also leads worship for his church, builds sets for special events, maintains websites for a few clients on the side, and hones his stand-up comedy routine at open-mike night.

The multi in multi-careering describes the entrepreneurial zeitgeist of our times, the cultural feeling that you're just one good idea away from success. Abby can be an admissions counselor and start a cake business. Gretchen can be an elementary school teacher and a floral designer. Gary can be a limo driver and contribute weekly movie reviews to a popular entertainment website.

A Life of Meaning, a Job That Makes a Difference

As any kid in a candy store will tell you, having more options results in more pressure. *How do you choose?* Multi-careering can be a little like that. After all, if the world is your oyster, then it's up to you to choose a job you love that fulfills you (and, if it doesn't, you can go find a new one). If a boring job is no longer some kind of given—a culturally accepted martyrdom to productivity, then you better figure out what you love to do and go after it!

LOOKING FOR SOME GOOD WORK

SUNDAY PAPER, 2014   JOBS EDITION

EXPECT WORK TO MAKE AN IMPACT*

- 37%
- 28%
- 23%
- 12%

- ● Yes, within 5 years
- ● Yes, in 6+ years
- ● Don't know
- ● No

"Having a job where I can make an impact is essential to my happiness"

53% of all adults

72% of graduating university students

*among graduating university students

All other things being equal, I'd take a 15% paycut …

(among graduating university students)

45% for a job that makes a social or environmental impact

58% to work for an organization with values like my own

Source: 2012 Net Impact study, "What Workers Want"

It's no longer enough for a job to pay the bills and occupy your time with good work. People demand jobs that *mean* something, that *change the world*, that *fulfill* them, and that they're *passionate* about. More than half of adults (53%) would, in fact, say it's essential to their happiness to have a job where they can make an impact. That number jumps to nearly three-quarters (72%) when you ask graduating university students. Adults rank having a job they're passionate about (39%) as more important than having one that offers financial security (33%) or funds their personal life (28%). Graduating university students say they would go so far as to take a 15% pay cut for a job that makes a social or environmental impact (45%) or to work for an organization with similar values to their own (58%).

Offering meaning, purpose, fulfillment, and change-the-world impact? That's a lot to ask of a job. Perhaps that's why 46% of adults feel anxious about choosing their career for fear they'll make the wrong choice. Or

ADULTS WANT A JOB THEY'RE PASSIONATE ABOUT

- Passion: **39**%
- Financial security: **33**%
- Funds personal life: **28**%

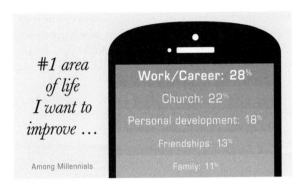

#1 area of life I want to improve ...

Among Millennials

Work/Career: 28%

Church: 22%

Personal development: 18%

Friendships: 13%

Family: 11%

why Millennials rank their career as their number one area for improvement.

Calling or Career?

Where does faith fit into all this? Do Christians believe their work is part of God's purpose or calling on their life? While more than three-quarters of Americans (77%) — Christian or otherwise — say they desire to have a purpose for living, only one in five say they have a clear sense of what God wants for their life. Among practicing Christians, this number doubles (41%). Even so, about one-third of employed Christians have never thought about their work as something they were called to. Only one in three practicing Christians say they feel called to their current work. And an alarming 48% of Christian Millennials think God is calling them to different work, but they haven't been willing to make the change.

With three-quarters of adults saying they're on the hunt for ways to live a more meaningful life and more than half (56%) wanting to make a difference in the world, marrying vocation to faith is an important step for many Christians. Yet nearly two-thirds (63%) of churched adults say they have not received any teachings in the last three years that helped shape their views on work or career. The church certainly has a rich tradition of helping people understand how vocation fits within God's greater work in the world. Today's multi-careering reality is one that will demand a revived focus on those teachings to help Christians understand and practice a more holistic idea of identity and calling.

The Multi-est of Them All

Answering these deeply personal and theological questions about vocation, calling, and purpose is no easy thing. Our goal in this FRAME is to help you begin to sort through some of those questions for your own life as you navigate this new economic and vocational landscape. It's also why we invited Bob Goff to be our guide.

Perhaps no one knows multi-careering better than Bob Goff, who makes it look easy. He is, among other things, an attorney, the founder of a human-rights organization (Restore International), the Honorary Consul for the Republic of Uganda to the United States, an adjunct professor at Pepperdine University and Point Loma Nazarene University, and the best-selling author of *Love Does*. He also started his own airline simply because DeHavilland Beaver seaplanes are really, really cool.

In this multi-careering life, there's no single path for everyone. Identifying the lifestyle you want, the career options in front of you, and the ways God has uniquely created you are crucial to traveling your journey well.

So here's to the adventure! ◆

MULTI-CAREERING

Do Work That Matters at Every Stage of Your Journey

THE FRAME

BY BOB GOFF

I'm a lawyer. I hate to introduce myself as a lawyer, though, because then you might assume I'm a sneaky guy who never returns phone calls. Maybe even worse things would come to your mind—but they shouldn't. The fact is, I'm not a sneaky guy at all, and I love to talk to people on the phone.

But, of course, I wasn't always a lawyer. Everybody has a first crummy job story, and I had my first crummy job when I was fifteen years old. I worked the graveyard shift in the parking lot of the San Jose airport. My job was to write down every license plate number on every car in the lot. Crazy, right? The idea was that if someone said they'd just pulled in an hour ago and had lost their parking ticket, the guy in the booth could look up the license plate number and see the car had actually been there for two weeks.

But this was my first job in justice. I was fighting crime even before I had my driver's license I suppose.

I've had more than one crummy job. And if you're like most people, you have too. We all threw newspapers or raked lawns or painted houses or babysat the Miller kids down the street. We worked at fast-food restaurants or delivered pizzas. But these were all just *jobs*. They were a way to stay busy and make a couple of bucks. None of us felt like those jobs defined who we were or represented the sum total of our contribution to the world.

And yet, crummy jobs shape us. Bad jobs early on can make for great careers later because they shape the way we see ourselves and our place in the world. We can draw on what we experience over a long, hot summer cleaning a camp kitchen to help us decide what we want for the rest of our lives. When we're young, a bad job can be all the wake-up call we need to pursue more education and a better job.

What gets confusing along the way is defining what is *better*. More cash, not just minimum wage, is better. But most of us want more than more money. We want more meaning. We want our jobs to matter. And not just matter in a theoretical sense; we (and 56% of us say this) want to make a difference in the world. We want our work to *really* matter to us, to our families, and to the world.

We are all meant to work. We are meant to contribute to our family and to our community and to our society in some fashion. Some people will do great work in the marketplace and others will do great work at home raising their families. A few will do a great job at both. It is the wisest among us who keep choosing to make a career out of raising our families, whether or not we have another job. I've seen my wife, Sweet Maria Goff, do just that. She's smart, she's beautiful, and she's fun. She could have done virtually anything in the marketplace, but she has made a career out of raising our family instead, and she'll be remembered for that for the next hundred years. Probably longer. By the time she's done, she will have had several careers. Having raised our family, she'll next play her part in raising our grandchildren. She's so vibrant, she'll probably have a hand in raising our great grandchildren.

There are times when I've wanted to return to the

PRIORITIES, PRIORITIES

Americans would rank their retirement priorities as follows:

45%
Enjoy life

17%
Relax

16%
Spend time with others

11%
Travel

7%
Do more fulfilling work

4%
Volunteer

simplicity of that first job writing down license plate numbers in the parking lot. However, it has been far more interesting, and far more meaningful, to have had several careers. When people ask my kids what I do for a living, they just laugh and walk away. They don't even know anymore. Frankly, I don't either. I grew up thinking people have one job, that one thing you do until you retire. But I've come to think differently about careers over time.

Being a lawyer has been one of my careers, but I've had many. I think the reason I've had many careers is that, just like you, I've continued to change over time. I think we were made to do many things. As our lives change, as we change, we will also change what we do. Some of us will do many things all at once. Others will do many things in a row. However the details shake out for you, set your sights high for all the things you do, in whatever order you do them. You'll most likely hit what you're aiming at.

Choose Your Life, Backfill Your Career

At some point, most people begin what they call a "career." I'm not really sure what makes us distinguish between what we call a job and what we call a career. To me, a career sounds like a job you do for long enough that you start to identify a part of yourself with it. That's not necessarily a bad idea—but it's not necessarily a good one, either. Some people think of what they do as merely work, while others think of it as legacy.

As time has passed, I've come to think of my careers as *a part* of my legacy, but certainly not all of it. After we're gone, those closest to us may appreciate the work we did, but they're more likely to remember how we did it. They will remember us for our love and whimsy. Only strangers will remember us just for our jobs or titles. The people for whom we care most and who care most for us will remember best how we loved them (or didn't) with our careers.

I wrote a book called *Love Does*. I struck a deal with a terrific publisher, Thomas Nelson, that I would trade writing a book for them for their building a school in northern Uganda. I wasn't sure the book would be any good, but I really wanted them to build that school, so I did my best. Then it hit the *New York Times* best-seller

WHAT YOU DO
≠
who you are

"What do you do?" It's often the first question we ask. So does our meaning come from our jobs? Most adults would say "no." When asked what's central to their identity, adults rank career last.

63%
FAMILY

46%
PERSONAL INTERESTS

39%
FAITH

34%
FRIENDS

32%
CAREER

Among 18-to-34-year-olds

list for quite a while, which was great because I got to share with a heap of readers about some of the things that excite me most.

I am not an author. Sure, I wrote a book—so, technically speaking, I guess I am an author. But let's not get technical. What I mean is, what I do isn't who I am. You know who I am? Sweet Maria's husband. Lindsey, Richard, and Adam's dad. I have learned to be very careful how I describe myself, because people do best at what they identify with most. That's why I'm glad to hear our FRAMES respondents ranked career last on the list of factors central to their identity— and that they ranked family first. Because how we identify ourselves is the thing we will become.

If we call ourselves speakers or writers or knife throwers but then some night we do a lousy job of speaking or writing or knife throwing, it's not just a bad night. It's an identity crisis. I've chosen to identify myself by Jesus, by my family, and by my friends. Do a great job at your family and you always win. Define yourself by them. When you're choosing what job to do, remember—it's not who you are, its a day job.

Some of us labor under an oppressive misconception. Far more limiting than a physical challenge, it's an impediment we make up ourselves. It's as simple as it is insidious. It is believing the lie that our titles and accomplishments have a significant shelf life. To be sure, getting a doctorate is a real accomplishment. But years from now, ask the family of the person with the PhD what comes to mind when you say her name; I'll bet you dollars to donuts they don't mention her big degree. I've won law cases worth hundreds of millions of dollars, and I'll bet you every cent that, decades from now, my kids won't remember a single case. Me neither.

We're not defined by our jobs. We're defined by our love.

Too many people choose their careers and then backfill their lives. That's a big problem if our careers are not, in the end, what define us. What if, instead, we choose our lives and backfill our careers? Here's what I mean: When you're choosing what you're going to do for a living, pick something that serves rather than competes with your lifestyle. I'm not smart enough to be a doctor, but if I were, I wouldn't be a dermatologist. You know why? Dermatologists have to be where the skin is. Lawyers don't. If you have a cell phone, you're in business. My lifestyle is on the move, and I like it that

TOP TEN FACTORS ESSENTIAL TO MY IDEAL JOB

01: 88%
Work/life balance

02: 88%
Positive culture

03: 87%
Good compensation

04: 86%
Interesting work

05: 86%
Job security

06: 78%
Ability to learn and grow

07: 76%
My opinions are valued

08: 67%
Employer has similar values

09: 61%
Flexible work hours

10: 53%
Contribution to society

Source: 2012 Net Impact study,
"What Workers Want"

way. I'd be bored if I were stuck in one place. Some people grow where they're planted, but some rot. Figure out who you are, where you flourish, and what lifestyle you want. Then go choose a career or three that help you get there.

When you're choosing your next day job, pick where you want to live first. I have an office in Seattle, but I live in San Diego. My Seattle office is at the top of a big high-rise. It has plenty of expensive vases and long tables. But I also have a small office in San Diego over a bakery. A bakery? You bet. Know why? I want everyone who comes to visit to feel welcome— and they do, because nothing smells more like welcome than fresh-baked bread. (You can tell I've been downstairs to that bakery a lot. I've been down there so many times, I jiggle when I walk.)

Take your current career or your next one and plant it where you want to grow. My office in San Diego is a three-minute walk from my house — two minutes if I run. Why? Because three minutes is how close I want to be to Sweet Maria and the kids. I spent years trying to get Sweet Maria to like me, and I want to be near that girl.

I spent even longer wanting to be a dad someday; I wanted to be available to the kids. You can do the same thing.

Living in San Diego and working in Seattle means I fly a lot. I've been commuting from San Diego to Seattle for a quarter of a century. Is that crazy? I don't think so. Sweet Maria drops me off at the airport in the morning, I go to work, and I'm usually home for supper. It's a two-hour flight, and I use the time to listen to great music. It's not hard work. Doing push-ups all the way to Seattle and back would be hard work. (Man, I'd be totally ripped.) I simply decided I'd choose my lifestyle and backfill where I work. I like being a lawyer in Seattle, where there is a more collegial feel than in Southern California, where we seemed to argue over whether water is wet. This isn't a jab at Southern California or an indictment of the lawyers there; it's just that lawyering in Southern California didn't work for me but living there did. So I changed things up so practicing law could work for me — and where we lived could work for my family.

What would it look like for you to do the same? Riff on your career. But do it in the key of Jesus and your family will be much better for it.

Find Your Thing

When I was growing up, every guy who had a guitar knew how to play the opening riff to "Stairway to Heaven." (YouTube it, kids.) Guitar stores everywhere started putting up red circles with lines through "Stairway to Heaven." It had been played into the ground first by every AM radio station and then by every beginning guitar player trying to impress a girl. But I wanted to do something not everyone knew how to do. That's why I chose the field of law. Among other reasons, I knew if I became a lawyer I could choose the kind of law I practiced and, by doing so, choose my lifestyle. By that, I don't mean choosing maids and butlers and chefs. I mean choosing how I spent my time, including how much of it I spent at home.

I'm a pretty good lawyer. I have been for a long time. There are all kinds of lawyers: criminal lawyers, divorce lawyers, antitrust lawyers. You know what I chose? Construction law. Know why? Simple. It isn't packed with emotion. There's a problem with a high-rise. It leaks. We figure out how to get it fixed. It's all about dirt and two-by-fours. I've never driven home worried about a high-rise. If I'd chosen another area of the law—one that demanded a lot of emotional involvement, one I would bring home with me every night—I'd probably be chronically tired, a bad husband, and a disengaged father. Here's my point: Once you find a career, find the space within that career that uniquely fits you. Having a bunch of window washers for high-rise buildings who are afraid of heights isn't going to be of much help to anyone. They need to either find first-floor windows to wash or change careers. The same is true for you. If what you're doing isn't you anymore—quit.

I was a partner at a big law firm. When our kids were the size of trout, I wanted, honestly, just to keep them alive. But as they got bigger, they learned how to talk and started to get interesting, and I wanted to hang out with them. A lot. I wanted to get to know them. I wanted to learn from them. I wanted to get into mischief with them. So one Friday in the early summer I told my twenty law partners that I was going to spend the next couple of months with my family at our place in Canada. They looked at me like I had walked in carrying a yellow umbrella and wearing snowshoes. They shook their heads in unison and reminded me how the sabbatical program worked: After ten years, I'd get fifteen minutes off.

I didn't argue with them. But on Monday, I wasn't there. I was in Canada with my family. I'm not kidding. A couple of months later, I came back. You couldn't imagine a bunch of people could get more bent out of shape than those partners were with me, until the next summer when I did the same thing.

Was that irresponsible? Perhaps. But it wasn't as irresponsible as it would have been for me to miss out on the lives of this terrific family of mine. If you needed dialysis on Tuesday, would you miss it because someone wanted you to be at work instead? Of course not. I need my family, and you need yours. So many of us wait until we're older to choose family—thinking once things get stable, we'll spend more time with them. Or once we retire we'll spend more time with our family.

WHERE DO YOU SPEND YOUR TIME?

Not surprisingly, people spend more time at work when they are young and shift their commitments as they age.

20s
MILLENNIALS

30 – 40s
GEN-XERS

50 – 60s
BOOMERS

68+
ELDERS

- ○ Work
- ○ Family
- ● Personal Development
- ● Friendships
- ● Church

You see it in how people answered our FRAMES questions — Millennials and Gen Xers are spending most of their time at work. Elders are spending their time with family. Pretty much everybody says when they retire they'll spend most of their time with family (76%).

But why wait so long? If you choose a career and give it everything you've got, maybe you win and maybe you lose. But if you choose your family and backfill your career behind it, you win every time. Choose them over and over, and you know what? When you're older, they'll choose you back and you'll never run out of things to talk about.

You know what most young people told us is their top area for improvement? Work. You know what aging boomers said is their top area for improvement? Family. So what if we focused more on our family when we're young? Maybe it wouldn't need so much improvement when we're older.

I haven't always gotten this right. One evening after having gone overseas to save the whole world (or so I thought), I pulled back into our driveway. Sweet Maria had put a Help Wanted sign in the window. I sat in the car and cried. She was telling me in the gentlest way possible that I must be present to win with my family. You do too. Don't make your family get out the Help Wanted sign. Try not to make them get it out even once. But if they do, make it your goal never to have them get it out again.

When I started what I would conservatively call my fourth career, I stopped carrying around business cards. If I gave someone a business card that said I was a lawyer, they might think

Areas of Improvement
As people get older, their priorities shift, as do the areas they feel need growth.

WORK/CAREER
	28%
	22%
	11%
	3%

PERSONAL DEVELOPMENT
	18%
	20%
	17%
	16%

FAMILY
	11%
	18%
	23%
	20%

FRIENDSHIPS
	13%
	15%
	14%
	16%

CHURCH
	22%
	18%
	19%
	27%

● Millennials   ● Gen-Xers
○ Boomers   ● Elders

KNOW THYSELF

Understanding who you are,
what you want, and what
you're good at is critical.

"I DON'T REALLY HAVE A GOOD SENSE OF MY STRENGTHS AND WEAKNESSES"

"I HAVE CLEAR GOALS FOR WHERE I WANT TO BE IN 5 YEARS"

"I'M CONFIDENT IN MY CURRENT LIFE CHOICES"

- Strongly agree
- Somewhat agree
- Somewhat disagree
- Strongly disagree

I wanted to be *their* lawyer. Chances are also good they might see me *only* as a lawyer. It's understandable, really. Most people turn, at least a little bit, into whatever their job title is. But if we're just us, we'll let our lives define our careers instead of the other way around.

If I carried a card for every career, I would look like the guy in the movie *Bourne Identity* with twenty different cards and identities, and that might really confuse people. All I've ever aimed for in life is to be helpful. So, for the last many years, I've carried around business cards that say just that: "Helpful." That's it. No status, no title, no career. Just helpful. Giving out those cards reminds me who I am and the legacy I want to leave behind. Now and after I'm gone, I want people to think of me as a big help.

All of my other careers—including being a part of my family and being a lawyer—are my efforts to be helpful. That's my thing. Helping.

What's your thing? What are you good at? What do you want to be remembered for? Once you've figured out the answers to those questions, it's a whole lot easier to make decisions about your careers.

Quitting Time

Just because we're not making it central to our identity doesn't mean career isn't significant. Career is, after all, where most adults report they spend the bulk of their time. So we shouldn't underestimate the importance of what we choose to do for a career or two or five. The choices we make about what we do are among the defining elements of our lives.

And yet, what we choose to quit is just as important. Don't be surprised if you need to quit a couple of jobs to

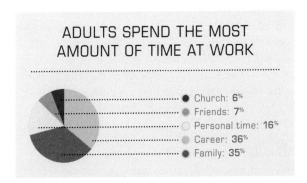

ADULTS SPEND THE MOST AMOUNT OF TIME AT WORK

- Church: **6**%
- Friends: **7**%
- Personal time: **16**%
- Career: **36**%
- Family: **35**%

find the right career—expect it. Some of us have careers that, at one time, served us and our ambitions. But over time those ambitions have changed and we've outgrown the career. When a career is no longer helping to shape who you're becoming, but is instead tying you to who you used to be, there's a fix.

Quit.

I quit things all the time. To be precise, I quit something every Thursday. Each week I pick one thing in my life to send to the scrap heap and, on Thursday, out it goes. Sometimes what I quit is perfectly good stuff. I do this because the pattern in my life tends to always by full. I can't squeak one more thing into my day. That's not good for a guy like me who puts a high value on spontaneity. So every week when Thursday comes around again, I quit something. Maybe you should too.

I also don't make appointments with anyone. As a lawyer, I found myself looking at a wall of appointments every day. I even started abbreviating my appointments: "I have an 8:00, a 9:15, a 2:00 p.m. . . ." Someone who does this is a person who's too busy making appointments with people to actually be with people. So I stopped. One Thursday, I quit appointments. Don't get me wrong, I don't just show up at the orthodontist's office unannounced and tell him to put braces on my kids. But I don't make appointments for myself anymore.

Now when I'm with people, I'm *with* them. There's plenty of time and breathing room to look each other in

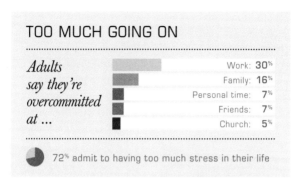

TOO MUCH GOING ON

Adults say they're overcommitted at ...

Work:	**30**%
Family:	**16**%
Personal time:	**7**%
Friends:	**7**%
Church:	**5**%

72% admit to having too much stress in their life

the eye and treat each other like human beings instead of like "an 8:00" or "a 9:15."

We could all stand to make some room and let God suck some terrific stuff into the space we create. It's amazing how a little elbow room can give us clarity about our choices and fresh perspective on our priorities. We accumulate activities and obligations like we're hoarders—because, actually, we are. We have stacks of things we keep doing just because they are familiar to us, not because they are meaningful for us. It's why so many of us (72%) feel stressed out and many of us admit to being overcommitted at work or even in our relationships.

So quit something. Try it. It will change your world. It will change your marriage. It will blow your mind. You may have things blocking your progress, blocking your family, even blocking your view of God. For goodness' sake, don't wait until Thursday. Don't have a Bible study about it. Just quit, right now. It will give both you and God some room to move around in your life. Sometimes the best way to fix something is to quit it.

When I was learning how to fly an airplane, I discovered I had a knack for it. I was pretty good at just about everything, but I was particularly good at takeoffs. I could get a plane in the air with almost no effort at all. It felt really natural to me. This mirrors my life. Getting an idea, even a career up and running is easy for me.

What took a little more practice was learning how to land. The first couple of times I tried to land on a runway, it felt less like I'd landed the plane and more like I'd been shot down. The reason, I discovered, is that I had a bad habit: I quit flying the plane about ten feet over the Tarmac. I needed to learn to fly the plane until the tires were on the ground. The fix for my landing problem wasn't to read more books about landing planes; the solution was to land planes more often.

I'm pretty good at landing now, I'm happy to report. Sure, I bounce the plane every now and again — and you may bounce too, with the next career you pick — but I've learned that landing is just as important as taking off. Landing one career and getting out of the plane is just as important as getting the next one off the ground.

If your present career can't take you where you want to go, look for a landing strip and just land the plane. Quit.

Making Adjustments

I got invited to an event at a guy's ranch in the Midwest. The friend who invited me said the ranch was sixty thousand acres and had a golf course and a number of magnificent buildings. Sure, I said. When do we go? Tomorrow, he said.

Tomorrow? *That's kind of short notice*, I thought, and then said so. I was certain he must have invited someone else and they had canceled. My friend came clean and admitted it. In fact, he continued, several guys he had invited had accepted the invitation and then canceled. One guy who is a successful doctor had been invited and then canceled three months ago. So my friend had invited another guy who is the CEO of a big company, and that guy had canceled the month before. So my friend invited another guy who heads up a huge nonprofit organization, but that guy had canceled just the day before. So my friend, who knew I say yes to almost everything and thought I would this time too, invited me at the last minute.

He was right, and off we went.

We flew to the nearest airport and then arrived at the ranch. I think the place was bigger than France. It was huge. When we got into the main building, there was a small book with the biographies of all the guys who had been invited for the weekend event. I forget what everyone had done but it was pretty impressive stuff. I think one guy had invented medicine—and he was the low achiever of the group. Thankfully, my biography was not included since all I had done was say yes to filling someone else's spot.

In the main room, I noticed a number of paintings hanging on the walls. I immediately recognized one huge six-by-four-foot canvas. I knew the painting because my grandmother had the exact same one on her wall when I was growing up. Hers was much smaller, and she got it for seven bucks at Target, frame included. I also noticed the painting here was tilted a little bit to the left. With my hands in my pockets, I watched as one of the other guests tried to be helpful by straightening it, lifting the bottom left corner of the frame with one little finger.

When he did, I jumped at the sound of alarms blaring through the building. From nowhere appeared men in suits with those radios that hang like Top Ramen noodles from their ears, like the guys in the Secret Service have. It was very cool.

Turns out, this was the original painting. It was wired through the wall to a state-of-the-art security system. My grandmother's copy from Target didn't come with that feature.

Some of us are afraid to make adjustments to our careers — sometimes it's a last-minute change to take advantage of an opportunity, like I did when I was invited to the retreat. But more likely there's a change we have been thinking about for some time. Somehow we've convinced ourselves if we make any changes, all the alarms will go off, and men in suits will appear out of nowhere to take us into custody. Yet most people who enjoy their careers make lots of adjustments along the way. Why? Because we all end up a little askew as time goes on. You were smart enough to start this career you have right now. Be smart enough to adjust it a little. If all the alarms go off, so what?

Some people approach everything they do like Olympic gymnasts. They want to leap from one high bar to the next, tuck into a couple of flips, stick the landing, and throw their arms behind their head in triumph. The fact is that most of us won't stick every landing. We'll end up sprawled on the mat more than once. Usually, though, we're the only ones keeping score. Give yourself a break. It's not the Olympics. It's a job. If you don't stick this one, stick the next one. Or at least get up and try again. Some people get too scared of falling to be much good to the world anymore. Don't let that be you.

Some of us don't get to that next job, to that next career, or to pursuing that next big ambition because we're afraid we'll fail. If we're honest, we'll admit that the pull our pride gives us to *look* good out-tugs our desire to *do* good. But at some point people who want to do more than one good thing with their lives accept the fact that failure isn't just part of the plan; it's much of the plan. And, accepting that fact, they're free to try new good things. They have clarity about their choices because fear of failure doesn't blind them to all the possibilities anymore.

They also expect a certain amount of pushback. They don't expect everything to go their way, and that makes them resilient and daring. If your definition of a bad day is losing an argument or losing your place in line or losing a job you're bored to death doing, you probably won't dare to do as much as the person who thinks a bad day is losing a battle with cancer or losing a friend. People with a healthy perspective on priorities — on what's most important — are nearly unstoppable.

Choose Well, but Choose

Even though I've been flying planes for years, I'm still a little timid about talking on the radio to the tower. Somehow I've got myself convinced I need to sound as good as the people in the control tower or the pilots flying the Boeing 747s. Listening to how fast they talk, I can't help but feel incompetent. I'm telling you this as a guy who talks really fast. But those others … The words are almost unintelligible, but it doesn't matter. You can tell they're pros who are cool as ice under pressure.

I asked a buddy who has a lot more experience than me if he understands what the controllers in the tower are saying. I was surprised when he said that, oftentimes, he doesn't understand most of the words — he just knows in advance what they would be saying to him at that point in the flight. Knowing what needs to happen next helps him decipher what they are saying to him about his next move.

Most of us have enough life experience by now to use this method to direct our careers. A good bit of the time, you know what the next move should be and I do too. So let's just make it without waiting for every single thing to make perfect sense.

You will leave one or more careers because you've changed. You'll leave another because you discover you're not very good at it. Perhaps you'll leave one or two because you fouled up and failed, and maybe you even got fired. When all is said and done, you'll probably leave as many jobs as you get. You may stop working before those scales are balanced, but only because death will be your career-ending move. We're all standing on level ground in this respect. So make your career choices often and make them well. Don't stare at the walls that seem to keep you from getting to the next career. Climb over them or tunnel under them, but see what is on the other side. Be more afraid of failure by watching than failure by trying.

I went to the optometrist recently. I sat down in the exam chair, and he fired up a machine with as many lenses as a gum ball machine has gum balls. He had me look into the first set of lenses and then flipped to a second set. He asked, "Which one is better? This? Or this?" You know the drill. You've probably sat in that chair as often as I have.

But I'm a lawyer, among other things, and one of the side effects of taking the bar exam in several states is that everything seems like a test to me. Lawyers like to be right — even when we're not. So I carefully told my optometrist which lenses helped me see more clearly, confident I had given the correct answer. But he asked the same question over and over and kept switching lenses. "This? Or this? This? Or this? This? Or this?" As we went on, over the next thiry minutes, the letters got clearer. By the end, the difference between one set of lenses and the next had become so small that it was hard

FAITHFUL AT WORK
(among Christian Millennials)

48% "God is calling me to different work, but I haven't made the change"

31% "I feel called to my current work"

26% "The work I am doing is helping to create a better world"

to tell which was better. Still I labored to give the right answer. "This one ... no, wait, that one ... no, wait, the other one." The difference between the lenses was vanishing. "This one" and "that one" were both pretty good.

When it comes to making career(s) decisions, some of us get wrapped around the axle — paralyzed — trying to make a choice between pretty good options. "This one ... no, wait, that one ... no, wait, the other one." Yet God has been exposing us to people and experiences our entire lives. We've made countless adjustments and mental notes about what we're better at, what we're worse at, and what we can see ourselves doing in the future. And still it's easy to get stuck between a couple of awfully good choices. That's probably why nearly half of us (46%) say we're afraid of making the wrong career choices. And it's probably why about the same number of Christian Millennials (48%) are afraid to change their jobs even when they *know* God is calling them to do something different. So maybe, rather than sitting paralyzed in the exam chair, laboring over differences only we can see, maybe we should just call it good, get out of the chair, and buy some frames and go see what's next.

It often takes more work to do nothing than it does to do a lot. Stalling, worrying, and hemming and hawing take a lot of energy that could be spent doing something terrific. You could spend your life making macaroni art projects because you're anxious about building the rocket ship that was supposed to be your life. Just build the rocket ship.

No Comparison

It's hard not to compare ourselves to other people and hold our work up to unrealistic expectations for how our career should have turned out. But comparison is a thief, and it will rip you off every time. When I'm tempted to compare myself to others and where they are headed, it seems like everyone except me has found their seat on the plane ride to success, happiness, and

Am I a disappointment?

THREE IN TEN ADULTS WORRY THEY'VE DISAPPOINTED THOSE CLOSE TO THEM WITH THEIR LIFE CHOICES

Percentage	Group
33%	Millennials
35%	Gen-Xers
29%	Boomers
20%	Elders

immeasurable riches. I can hear the flight attendant saying, "Now boarding all passengers ... except you."

Some people seem to have more options than others, but I think it's more likely that we simply all have different options than each other. The farmer who spends countless sunbaked hours coaxing a crop from the soil, tending animals, and mending fences may have less time than a freelance writer to ruminate about a different career path or the possibility of having multiple careers. So too the single mother of three who has chronic medical problems or the person with a physical impairment that limits the activities he can do. All these folks can and do ask the same questions about meaning and work and fulfillment and legacy, but the list of viable options for each of them is different. Not necessarily shorter, just different.

At some point we need to admit that we are not each other. You're not your dad or mom, your old boyfriends or girlfriends, your roommates or colleagues. You're just wonderful old you, and I'm just marvelous old me.

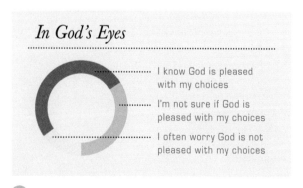

In God's Eyes

I know God is pleased with my choices

I'm not sure if God is pleased with my choices

I often worry God is not pleased with my choices

Don't lose the scent of your next career by following the trail of someone else's. When we try to be someone else, it usually comes off like a bad Elvis impression: painful for everyone and a bit pitiful. And the worst part is we won't be sure who we are anymore.

When it comes down to it, the only person we should compare ourselves to is Jesus. Instead of measuring ourselves against the success, happiness, and wealth of others, let's measure ourselves against his joyful, relentless love. Whatever it is you do, give your love away freely. Give away so much of it that it looks like you're made of the stuff. In the reverse economy of Jesus, the more extravagant you are with your love, the less it's wasted. This will hold true in your life and your careers.

Do (Some of) What You Love

I got a job as an accountant out of college. I'm not really sure why. I think someone told me accounting was a great thing because it is secure and predictable. The problem was and is this: I don't want much security and predictability. It's not who I am. Having everything planned out in advance is like oxygen to some people but like torture to me. I was listening to people who loved me and wanted good things for me, but they didn't know me. They didn't see who I was becoming as a young man.

We need to be careful about who we give the microphone to. I was onstage with a foreign dignitary once, interviewing him in front of an audience. I was holding the microphone in front of me when I asked the questions and then in front of him as he answered. Things were going well until I made the huge mistake of handing him the microphone. It was no longer my microphone. It was *his* microphone. I knew we were in trouble when he started out by saying, "I really don't have much to say …" My clothes went out of style halfway through his talk.

Be careful about who you give the microphone to when you're choosing your next career. It's your microphone. It's not theirs unless you give it to them. Surround yourself with wise people. Listen to what they have to say. But hang on to the microphone.

I've always been fascinated by DeHavilland Beaver seaplanes. They take off and land on the water. They're *guy* planes. They're big. They're tough. They'd be made out of beef jerky if someone could make beef jerky planes fly.

We have a place far up at the end of an inlet in Canada. We've been going there for decades now. Early on, we would hire a Beaver seaplane to fly us in. I remember thinking two things to myself on one of the trips. First, I'd sure like to fly this thing, and second, I bet the guy won't let me. I was right about the first and wrong about the second. A minute after I asked, I was flying the Beaver. I was hooked.

The plane flew away after dropping us off, and my mind's wheels were spinning. Hey, I'm a lawyer, I thought. I bet I could start an airline. I must have been mumbling aloud because Sweet Maria heard and asked, "An airline? You're going to start your own airline?"

Yes, I said. And I held out my arms and flew around the room.

I filled out all the paperwork with Transport Canada and within the year we were good to go — except for one last thing. They said I needed a plane before I could become an airline. Shoot.

The thing about Beaver airplanes is that they made a lot more of them than are still flying today. That's because people fly them in and out of small lakes and hit things, like trees and the shore. We used this to our advantage and got the wings from one crashed Beaver, the fuselage from another, and the pontoon floats from still another. All that was left was to pick some colors and paint our new plane. I was sitting in a Krispy Kreme donuts shop (I know, I know … it's the only time I've ever been there, honest), looking at a box of donuts, and I had an idea. I'd steal Krispy Kreme's colors, their font, everything, and paint the plane to look like a box of donuts. So that's what I did.

Now we had our airline. We had a ticket agent. We had a dock guy. The problem was that we didn't have any passengers. When one finally bought a thirty-dollar ticket and got into my flying donut box for a ride, it was like I was tearing up hundred-dollar bills and throwing them into the propeller. We needed more customers to fill this plane. I needed a new idea or this next career was going to crash.

So this is what we did. We loaded the plane every morning with fresh fruit and newspapers and flew into every logging camp in British Columbia to deliver them. Within six months, we owned all the business in every inlet. We were the guys who flew the plane that looked like a donut box, and we were nice guys to boot. Within six months we had ten planes and were flying a hundred or more trips a day, including several into Vancouver International Airport.

Sometimes all you need is a big idea. You don't even need a donut box (but it helps). Pursue your ideas with joy and whim and determination. Then stand back and see what God makes of them.

Everything you love doesn't need to be a career. In fact, if you make a career out of some of the things you love, you won't love them anymore. What you can do, though, is have several careers at the same time and do lots of things. Viable careers will work and will take on a life of their own. Others won't work and will fade away. Someone once told me they thought I was spread a mile wide and an inch deep. I think they were trying to say I had too much going on — and I agree that can be a problem for some people. I also think it depends on who you are. If you're an ice skater, water that's frozen solid an inch deep and a mile wide is perfect. If you're a high diver, not so much. The answer is to figure out who you are and what you're good at and then do a lot of that.

Here's a question worth considering. A lot of people choose their careers based on what they are *able* to do. I think the better question is this: What are you *made*

> *1/5 of adults have a clear sense of what God wants for their life*

34% of employed Christians have never thought about their work as something they were called to

to do? Some people are made to do one thing at a time. Some are made to do several things at the same time. Whether it's one thing or several things, do the things you were made to do. Only one out of five people told us they have a clear sense of what God wants them to do with their life. Some people refer to this as a "calling." I think that's a great concept, but I'm a guy who gets a lot of calls, and the ones I get go like this: My phone rings and I answer. To me, that's a call.

I use different terms to describe the nudges I've felt from God toward what I am made to do. I ask my friends and myself what I seem to be really good at. I ask myself what really lights me up. What makes me jump out of bed full of anticipation in the morning? What seems to be working—not just for me but also for everyone around me? Those are the things that make for a great life and great careers. That's a calling you can bank on.

The corollary to asking what you're good at can be just as useful to figure out your calling. What are you crummy at? What hasn't worked out very well in the past? Some people I've met tell me they're working really hard to be better at this thing they stink at. I want to shout, "Don't do it! Don't work on it at all!" A key to having one terrific career or several is to stop doing what you stink at. Unless you stink at relationships. If you do, get better at them.

When Careers Go Wrong

Not everything you try will work. That's okay. In fact, it's better than okay! Try again or don't try it ever again—you pick. They're both good choices.

I graduated from law school thinking about how Jesus dealt with conflict. If I were going to deal with conflict, I'd get the smartest, most powerful people I could find to help me out. But Jesus always did the opposite. He said to get the least of the brothers or sisters to solve it. Having barely made it into law school, I felt like I qualified as the least of the brothers. So shortly after graduating and passing the bar exam, I started the Christian Reconciliation Service. I put up a sign and waited for people to come pouring in.

It never happened.

Finally, two guys stumbled through the door one day. They were really bent out of shape with each other about a business deal that had gone south. I met with them a number of times, but we got nowhere. They were daggers for each other. But then I had an idea.

There was a boxing ring in a seedy part of town that I could rent for thirty-five dollars, including gloves and a referee. I told my clients we'd meet down there the following Thursday. These guys clearly didn't want to resolve anything; they just wanted to beat each other up. I figured we could skip the middle part, which wasn't working anyway, and go straight to the fight.

I showed up. The ref showed up. I even had a set of gloves on—I was so frustrated with these guys, I had decided I would take on the winner.

Neither guy showed up, and I've never heard from either of them again. I closed down the Christian Reconciliation Service at a net loss of thirty-five dollars. But here's what I gained: I figured out I'm lousy at getting people who don't want to reconcile with each other to reconcile with each other. Rather than years of frustration doing something I was lousy at, I decided to put a quick end to that career and practice construction law instead—which, as it happens, I'm good at.

I worked as a welder in high school. I didn't build aircraft carriers; I built foot-long, artsy-rustic crab boats to sell at swap meets. They were pretty ridiculous, but the occasional hoarder would come along and buy one. I got five dollars for each boat I made, which is big money for a teenager. As you might imagine, there was not a punishing level of intricate detail that went into each boat; I could crank out five or six per hour.

The guy I worked for—the guy with the swap-meet-crab-boat business—had an old MGB roadster. I always had my eye on that car. He knew this, and he offered to sell it to me. I didn't have any cash, so we negotiated a deal based on me making a lot of crab boats for him to sell. I think I owed him about a thousand crab boats.

Driving down the highway in my MGB, I was feeling pretty cool. I had the top down and an arm out the window. The wind was blowing through my hair, and I thought about how fast I could punch out those crab boats and actually own this thing.

Just then, the hood of the car flew off. It missed my head by about an inch and folded in half in the fast lane. I pulled over and stood up on the floorboard to get a better look at where the hood had landed. As I stood up, my foot went through the floorboard, which was just as rusted out as the bolts holding the hood on.

I wasn't feeling cool anymore. I felt like I'd been taken. I was embarrassed and ashamed. The worst part of it was that I still owed my boss, that crook, a thousand crab boats. I made boat after boat for months, shaking my head all the while, wondering how I could have been so foolish. Not just for buying a rusted-out MGB, but even more for being indebted to this guy for a car I couldn't afford.

I wish I hadn't been taken in the deal, but that experience shaped the way I've done business and run my careers ever since.

I have a law firm. We have an agreement that governs how the firm operates. It's a pretty simple deal, really. By written agreement, the firm dissolves every year. That's it. December 31 of every year, it's all over. I'm every father-in-law's worst nightmare. I'm out of work every year and have been for a quarter of a century.

But because we do this, we have tremendous freedom. I don't owe anyone a thousand boats anymore. I decide who gets paid what. When it comes to bonuses, the agreement says I give people whatever I want to give. Honest, that's what it says. If someone thinks I've been a tightwad, they only have to hang with me until December 31 and then the law firm is over. They can say *sayonara* and start their own law firm. There are no rusty floor boards.

Here's what I've learned from my experiences. I don't try to control people, and I don't want people to try to control me. In my firm, no one is angling for the best cases or extra credit for what they've done. We're all in it together. One of the best parts is that, with Sweet Maria's permission, I get to take a knee and propose to each person in the law firm to ask if they would do me the honor of practicing law with me for one more year. There's something special about being chosen, and it works both ways. We choose each other. We are all free and, as a result, we keep choosing each other.

I thought I wanted to do youth ministry. There was a terrific organization that helped high school kids all around the world. I wanted more than anything to help people consider matters about faith and life, so I raised my own support after graduating from college and asked if I could work for this terrific outfit. They said no.

No? But it won't cost you anything, I said. They had factored that in, they said. The answer was still no.

Defeated, I went to law school. Many years later, I was up near a camp that ministry outfit owned in British Columbia. I went to the organization and offered to have our attorneys and staff do for free the hundreds of thousands of dollars in legal work they were paying other lawyers to do. They said no—again.

No? But it won't cost you anything, I said. I put aside the fact that we are the smart guys people hire to check other people's work, and suggested they could have someone check our work. Nope. They didn't want us.

I wasn't mad; I was just confused. I thought to myself, this is something I'm really good at. I want to give away my time and no one wants me.

Here's the thing: Some of the things we pursue, even in our areas of expertise, just won't work out. I bet the same thing has happened to you once or twice. You really wanted something. It was not only something you were good at, but also something you thought you could help with. It was something you thought God had uniquely qualified you to do. And then you got a no. Some things will happen in our pursuit of a career that we just won't understand. What we do next matters more than all the no's put together.

I hadn't killed the law firm yet, so I decided every time something profitable happened at work, I'd buy some of the forest around that camp in British Columbia. For the next twenty years a lot of happy things happened, and I bought up the forest. What started out as an inexplicable set of no's ended up as a lodge on thousands of acres of land in Canada. What I thought would be a career that might help hundreds turned into a different career that has helped thousands. We invite people to come and consider matters of faith and life at the lodge. Lots of people. Many more, in fact, than if I'd received the yes I was looking for decades ago.

Sometimes we ask God what he wants us to do and we get a nudge about what it is. When we get a no, we're often puzzled. But what doesn't make sense at one point in time will make a lot of sense at some other point in the future.

I serve as the Honorary Consul for the Republic of Uganda, which means I get to connect a lot of Ugandans with Americans and help Ugandans out when they're in the United States. You're thinking, wait, Bob's not Ugandan. But you don't have to be a Ugandan to be a diplomat for Uganda, you don't have to be a pilot to own an airline, and you don't have to be a donut to own a donut shop. Sometimes, you just have to say yes.

The flag of Uganda flies over my house in San Diego. You know what that means? My house is in Uganda, not America. It's the diplomatic mission of another country. How cool is that? If you really mess up, you can come to my house and seek asylum.

Do you have a big ambition about what your next career will be? Some of us keep waiting for permission to do the things God said he made us to do. Being alive is all the green light you need. Go after that career that reflects who you're becoming.

I'm not really sure how I became Uganda's consul, it just kind of happened. And it might be the same for you with your next career. Someone will ask if you want to do something, and you will say yes or no. Go with yes as often as you can, but only if it makes sense with who you are becoming. If it adds to your life, if it brings whimsy to your life and the lives of the people you love, do it.

Especially if it means representing another country. You'll never have to pay another speeding fine. You'll have diplomatic immunity. What I've discovered is that you can pick what you start as a career and you can pick what you stop. But it's what you pick that tells a lot about where your life is going. ◆

MULTI-CAREERING

Do Work That Matters at Every Stage of Your Journey

RE/FRAME

BY SCOTT HARRISON

Not only is Scott Harrison the visionary at the helm of one of the most innovative charities today, but he's also a fascinating example of one of the most incongruous career changes the world of start-ups has ever seen.

Today, many know Scott as the founder and CEO of charity: water, the nonprofit organization with the outrageous goal of bringing safe and clean drinking water to every single person on the planet. But before that, he was in the business of a wholly different kind of drink. As a New York City nightclub promoter for ten years, Harrison's career consisted of late nights, loud music, and luxe cocktails. But when he realized something as simple as clean water is a luxury many around the world cannot afford, he began to question his career path. That, combined with a rediscovery of his childhood faith, led Scott to leave his glamorous job and start something new—something he felt could make a real difference in the world.

Harrison is no stranger to multi-careering, and he's not alone. For the new wave of entrepreneurs, moonlighters, and multi-career professionals, here's his advice on how to use those day job skills to your advantage, how to know when it's time to move on in your career, and what it really takes to pursue work that matters.

Q *Why do you think people today are going through more than one career in a lifetime?*

A People are searching for happiness and fulfillment through their work, and expect to find that in today's marketplace. It seems to me that to previous generations, work was work. It was something you "had" to do to support your family, and people looked forward to the weekends. TGIF had more meaning than today, as people [now] look for jobs they love. In the words of [business author] Daniel Pink, jobs that provide them with autonomy give them a chance at mastery and a purpose.

Q *Why are people less likely to stick with one company and one job?*

A I think it's simply a process of elimination for many people. They don't find what they are looking for, so they move on with continued expectations.

Q *How would you describe your own tipping point in the decision to make a pretty significant career change from NYC nightclub promoter to charity founder?*

A I basically got people wasted for a living. My legacy was going to be a life of meaningless parties that helped people escape. After coming back to a very lost Christian faith after ten years, I decided to explore a radical change and serve the poor. That led me to Liberia immediately following the fourteen-year civil war, and there, everything changed for me.

Q *What are the skills and lessons you learned in your first job that you needed for your work at charity: water? In other words, how did that first job prepare you for your work now?*

A I was a storyteller then, and I'm a storyteller now. But the story has changed.

The story I spent almost a decade telling was this, "If you can get past the velvet rope of our clubs ... If you bring the right people with you ... If you can spend fifteen dollars a cocktail or five hundred on a bottle of champagne, then your life has meaning. You are special and important." I was an includer, and used to love to stand in the DJ booth high over the party, watching the revelry.

Now, I'm telling a much different story. "There are 800 million people without access to clean water simply because of where they were born. We can do something about it. We can help create a world where every man, woman, and child has access to life's basic need. Consider this an invitation. It's a party where the entire world gets clean water. Do you want to come?"

Q *A lot of young, fresh-faced twentysomethings probably come up to you on a regular basis, asking, "I want to start a charity. What's the first step?" What is your response? Do you tell them to go for it, or do you have some cautionary words?*

A I normally encourage them to see if anyone else is doing what they are passionate about in a way that inspires them. To ask themselves what they uniquely can bring to the table. Can they innovate? Can they push the issue forward by thinking in a new way about an age-old problem? Can they inspire, lead, and get others to follow those new ideas? If the answer is yes, then they should go for it!

Q *Every job has its drudge work—even "dream" jobs. So how do we discern between the sort of inevitable weariness of hard work and the discontent that is perhaps a sign we should be moving on?*

A As charity: water has grown so rapidly, it's gotten incredibly more difficult. We've faced challenges we never even imagined in the beginning. At the moment, we've funded almost 10,000 water projects in twenty countries around the world. There are many different water solutions, a diversity of political and economic climates, and huge differences in culture. But as our growth has revealed greater complexity and challenges, I believe the organization has embraced the "hard" rather than run from it. Our amazing staff have brought the best of themselves—their creativity and passion—to solving these problems instead of running from them.

I think it's time to move on if your job doesn't challenge you anymore, if you stop learning from those above and beneath you, or if you don't believe in your company or organization's mission.

Q *Looking back, what do you wish you'd known then about what it takes to follow a dream and pursue work that matters?*

A I spent about 9.9 years too long in the nightlife industry, and I'm grateful I've been able to redeem some of that time and those skills learned in my current mission with charity: water. For me, those years were an act of rebellion and selfishness. I wish

I'd been more focused on serving others instead of myself.

Q *With the work that you do — important work that saves lives — it would seem difficult to separate your identity and worth from it. Has that been true for you?*

A As founder and CEO of an organization, it's difficult to separate your identity from your work sometimes, especially when people constantly refer to you as "that water guy." But I try to be mindful of my identity as a loved and valued son of God, a husband, and hopefully one day soon, a father!

Q *Some jobs just seem inherently more glamorous and meaningful. Most people, for example, likely agree providing clean water for those who don't have it is meaningful work. But what about those jobs that aren't in the spotlight or that don't seem so obviously "world changing" — software programming or factory worker or construction management — can we infuse our work with meaning in any day job, any career path, any side passion project?*

A Yes, and believe me, as leaders, we often have moments where we wish we could fade out of the spotlight, put our heads down, and do work quietly and without recognition or great responsibility that weighs so heavily sometimes. I believe that all work can be infused with meaning as long as it's done with integrity, respect, passion, and excellence.

Q *In a world of start-ups and "change the world" mantras, what words would you give to people to live meaningfully in more personal ways? In their families, neighborhoods, faith communities? Does our work always have to have global impact or otherwise we're just settling and being "boring and normal"?*

A I don't think meaningful work needs to have a global impact at all. I think living and working intentionally, being true to your values and doing everything you do with excellence, can take on so many forms. ◆

MULTI-CAREERING

Do Work That Matters at Every Stage of Your Journey

RE/FRAME

BY KEATON RANNOW

We often think of visionaries and innovators as forward-thinking people. After all, dreaming is about envisioning the future. But sometimes we remember our dreams best by looking back—all the way back to when we were kids, when people asked the inevitable: What do you want to be when you grow up?

Childhood is the time when we first start to dream, to imagine what our place in the world might be. To ask ourselves what that dream job will look like. To explore and discover what makes us come alive.

Take Keaton, for example. Keaton may only be ten, but he has clear plans for his life—from becoming a Lego architect to growing closer to God. And he's mapped it all out in the following PowerPoint presentation. Not surprisingly, Keaton's got plans to lead the multi-careering life.

But Keaton's not waiting until he grows up. After learning who Bob Goff is and what he does, Keaton asked that his writing honorarium for this book be donated to Bob Goff's organization Restore International—because you are never too young to find work that matters.

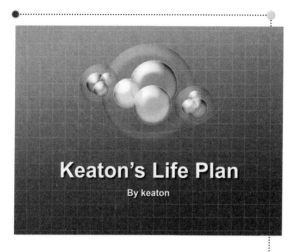

Keaton's Life Plan

By keaton

My 10 life goals

- 1. Grow up to be a nice Christian man
- 2. Get a nice wife
- 3. Get a good job, one that I like
- 4. Have two kids (each boys two years apart)
- 5. Grow as close as I can get to God
- 6. Make more and more friends as I grow
- 7. Work hard in school
- 8. Believe in God wherever I go
- 9. Teach my kids about God and help them live their lives as best as they can
- 10. Do not give up in life

My wife

- A Christian woman, humorous, hard working, caring, energetic, strong when hurt, is a leader, likes to help others, and doesn't care what others think.

Warning: No one person can be all these things.

Possible jobs

- Engineer, architect, hockey player, Lego designer at Lego land California or at Florida

Places to live

- Minnesota, Florida, Indiana, Michigan, Colorado, Pennsylvania, Washington, Georgia, and South Carolina

....

- What do you think about Bob Goff's insistence that failure is a necessary part of career success? Is fear of failure holding you back from a new career direction?

- Where does your family rank in your priorities? What would it look like to move them to the top of your list?

- Do you believe God has called you to your current career(s)? How do you know? Is he also calling you to something else?

- How do you define career success? How will you know when you've made it?

- What are you good at? What do you love doing? What gets you up in the morning, excited to start the day? What career encompasses your answers to these questions?

- Think about the balance in your life right now. Where do you feel out of balance? Where do you feel overcommitted? What could you quit today (or next Thursday)?

- What makes you still feel childlike wonder? How could you pursue that curiosity—whether as a career or as a side pursuit?

FRAMES started with the idea that people need simple, clear ideas to live more meaningful lives in the midst of increasingly complex times. To help make sense of culture, each FRAME includes major public-opinion studies conducted by Barna Group.

If you're into the details, the research behind the *Multi-Careering* FRAME included one thousand surveys conducted among a representative sample of adults over the age of eighteen living in the United States and its territories. This survey was conducted from July 29, 2013, through August 1, 2013. Additionally, 1,005 phone interviews were conducted from June 25, 2013, through June 29, 2013, with a 96% incidence rate and a 79% cooperation rate. The sampling error for both surveys is plus or minus 3 percentage points, at the 95% confidence level.

Multi-Careering also includes survey results from original Barna Group research conducted for Brad Lomenick's book *The Catalyst Leader* (Thomas Nelson, 2013). Used with permission.

If you're really into the research details, find more at www.barnaframes.com.

ABOUT BARNA GROUP

In its thirty-year history, Barna Group has conducted more than one million interviews over the course of hundreds of studies and has become a go-to source for insights about faith and culture. Currently led by David Kinnaman, Barna Group's vision is to provide people with credible knowledge and clear thinking, enabling them to navigate a complex and changing culture. The company was started by George and Nancy Barna in 1984.

Barna Group has worked with thousands of businesses, nonprofit organizations, and churches across the country, including many Protestant and Catholic congregations and denominations. Some of its clients have included the American Bible Society, CARE, Compassion, Easter Seals, Habitat for Humanity, NBC Universal, the Salvation Army, Walden Media, the ONE Campaign, SONY, Thrivent, US AID, and World Vision.

The firm's studies are frequently used in sermons and talks. And its public-opinion research is often quoted in major media outlets, such as *CNN*, *USA Today*, the *Wall Street Journal*, Fox News, *Chicago Tribune*, the *Huffington Post*, the *New York Times*, *Dallas Morning News*, and the *Los Angeles Times*.

Learn more about Barna Group at www.barna.org.

THANKS

....

Even small books take enormous effort.

First, thanks go to Bob Goff for his heartfelt and inspiring work on this FRAME — offering his trademark whimsy, years of experience, and lessons from a life well lived to create what we pray is a prophetic and encouraging look at how to live a life shaped by God's callings and priorities.

We are also incredibly grateful for the contribution of Scott Harrison and Keaton Rannow, one for his thoughtful retrospective and one for his grand dreaming ... and both for their earnest consideration of God's guidance in their lives.

Next, Barna Group gratefully acknowledges the efforts of the team at HarperCollins Christian Publishing, especially Chip Brown and Melinda Bouma for catching the vision from the get-go. Others at HarperCollins who have made huge contributions include Jennifer Keller, Kate Mulvaney, Mark Sheeres, and Shari Vanden Berg.

The FRAMES team at Barna Group consists of Elaina Buffon, Bill Denzel, Traci Hochmuth, Pam Jacob, Clint Jenkin, Robert Jewe, David Kinnaman, Jill Kinnaman, Elaine Klautzsch, Stephanie Smith, and Roxanne Stone. Bill and Stephanie consistently made magic out of thin air. Clint and Traci brought the research to life — along with thoughtful analysis from Ken Chitwood. And Roxanne deserves massive credit as a shaping force on FRAMES. Amy Duty did heroic work on FRAMES designs, from cover to infographics.

Finally, others who have had a huge role in bringing FRAMES to life include Brad Abare, Justin Bell, Jean Bloom, Patrick Dodd, Grant England, Esther Fedorkevich, Josh Franer, Jane Haradine, Aly Hawkins, Kelly Hughes, Steve McBeth, Geof Morin, Jesse Oxford, Beth Shagene, and Santino Stoner.

Many thanks!

Share Your Thoughts

With the Author: Your comments will be forwarded to the author when you send them to *zauthor@zondervan.com*.

With Zondervan: Submit your review of this book by writing to *zreview@zondervan.com*.

Free Online Resources at
www.zondervan.com

Daily Bible Verses and Devotions: Enrich your life with daily Bible verses or devotions that help you start every morning focused on God. Visit www.zondervan.com/newsletters.

Free Email Publications: Sign up for newsletters on Christian living, academic resources, church ministry, fiction, children's resources, and more. Visit www.zondervan.com/newsletters.

Zondervan Bible Search: Find and compare Bible passages in a variety of translations at www.zondervanbiblesearch.com.

Other Benefits: Register to receive online benefits like coupons and special offers, or to participate in research.